W0099680

World War I

Aaron Jolly and Rjurik Davidson

Series Editor **Rob Waring**

Level 6 - ❶

World War I

Aaron Jolly and Rjurik Davidson

© 2017 Seed Learning, Inc.

Series Editor: Rob Waring
Acquisitions Editor: Liana Robinson
Copy Editor: Casey Malarcher
Cover/Interior Design: Andy Roh

ISBN: 978-1-9464-5250-4

10 9 8 7 6 5 4 3 2 1
21 20 19 18 17

Contents

World War I

These days, war is sometimes seen as a glorious adventure. Television, books, and films often make war seem exciting with fights or great battle scenes. Soldiers are strong and brave heroes.

German soldiers shelter in a trench.

At the beginning of World War I (1914-1918), many people greeted the announcement of war with enthusiasm. Men volunteered to go and fight. The war brought out feelings of patriotism.

Most people, however, thought that the war would be over in a few months. In fact, no one could imagine the amount of death and destruction the war would cause.

Bandaged British soldiers during the war

Crowds gathered in Paris at the beginning of World War I.

ANCENIS NANTES

What Is a Trench?

A trench is a long ditch cut into the ground. Much of World War I (WWI) was fought using trenches. The trenches were usually built with wood and sandbags, and they were about two meters deep.

A German bunker, Flanders Fields

Trenches helped protect soldiers. They were usually cut in a zigzag pattern, to stop anyone shooting down the length of them. But the trenches could be miserable places with problems such as rats, flooding, and disease.

The safest places were the underground shelters called bunkers. Food and weapons were stored inside. Sometimes the soldiers slept on wooden benches in the bunkers.

Preserved trenches in Holland

Why Did WWI Start?

Why do countries go to war? In the case of WWI, there is a lot of debate. However, one event started it. An Austro-Hungarian prince was murdered on June 28, 1914. His name was Archduke Franz Ferdinand.

At that time, many countries were becoming powerful in Europe. Many of these countries wanted more colonies. They built up their armies in case they needed to fight with their neighbors.

Soon after the murder of Archduke Ferdinand, almost all of Europe was at war, as well as Russia, Turkey, Japan, and some British colonies like Australia. There were two opposing sides, the Allies and the Central Powers.

The street corner where the Archduke was killed

The arrest of Archduke Ferdinand's murderer

A New Way to Fight

Battles in previous wars happened fast. Armies moved quickly on horses. They covered a lot of ground. In WWI, this changed mostly because of trench warfare. As a result, battles became long and slow.

Preserved WWI trenches in Belgium

Allied and Central Power forces began digging the first trenches on the Western Front on September 15, 1914. Eventually, the trenches stretched right across Europe. In total, the trenches built during WWI would stretch about 25,000 miles if they were laid end-to-end.

German machine gunners in a trench

7

A German soldier ready to throw a grenade, in the background wearing a helmet

Soldiers wearing gas masks

Most trenches were terrible places to live. Often there was nothing to do. No wonder many soldiers lost hope or became depressed while they were stuck in the trenches.

Both sides tried to develop new weapons. Science and industry were put into the service of the war. Hot air balloons were used to scan the enemy's trenches. Grenades became important weapons. Large artillery guns on wheels could shoot the enemy from far away.

An American artillery gun in Beaumont, France

One of the worst weapons was poison gas. Without a gas mask, soldiers died horribly. The chlorine gas filled their lungs up with liquid until they drowned. After WWI, gas was banned for use in war.

Imagine the War

Can you imagine what it was like living in the trenches? Imagine you are standing there beside your friend, Johnny. It rained in the morning, so both of you are standing in water. In fact, Johnny has something called "trench foot." His feet have been wet for so long that they are rotting, but at least neither of you is sick like some of the other soldiers.

Out of the corner of your eye, you see something move. It's a rat! The rats are everywhere—nothing gets rid of them! It has been days since you have had a hot meal. You remember your favorite dinner from home, your bedroom, a hot shower . . . All of those things seem like a dream now!

Soldiers dying between the trenches

A German trench

Soldiers crossing no man's land

You and Johnny look toward the enemy trenches. The muddy area between the trenches is called "no man's land." It is filled with dead soldiers and rows of sharp barbed wire. There is no time to dig graves. The dead bodies smell horrible.

The enemy's trench is only 200 meters from yours. You keep your head below the top of the trench. You know that snipers are ready to shoot you if you show yourself.

You did not think you would be away from home this long. You thought the war would be different. Trenches and machine guns have changed things.

No man's land

![Soldiers outside the trench unprotected from gunfire]

Soldiers outside the trench unprotected from gunfire

That night, you and Johnny are part of a small raiding party. About thirty of you slowly crawl across no man's land on your stomachs. You have all blackened your faces so the Germans cannot see you coming. Your goal is to capture German soldiers for interrogation.

Soldiers creeping across no man's land

Suddenly, there is light in the sky. The Germans have fired a light-shell rocket. You dive into a deep mud puddle. A machine gun starts to fire. You hear Johnny scream. You wait until the light rocket burns out. When it is dark again, you rush to Johnny's side. He has been shot.

This was the story for many of those who fought in WWI.

Tanks in WWI

The tank was an important invention during WWI. The idea of the tank came from farm tractors, which could drive across muddy fields. WWI tanks were slow and noisy. They were like great rumbling, smoky beasts. They helped to capture enemy trenches, and they made war more mobile again.

The first tanks were used in the Battle of the Flers in 1916. In the first three days of the battle, the Allies advanced 2 km. The tanks were far from perfect, but the Allies thought they were useful. During the war, the British produced over 2,500 tanks. The French produced more than 3,500. The Germans were never really convinced that tanks were useful. They only produced 20 of them.

A WWI tank

A group of tanks close to the front line

The Battle of the Somme

One of the most famous battles of WWI was the Battle of the Somme in 1916. It was the most bloody battle of the war. The English thought they could beat the Central Powers for good.

It is hard to imagine how big the battle was and how many people were involved. The Allies began with an eight-day artillery gun attack. Then 750,000 men attacked, but the German defenses held. On the first day of the battle, 58,000 British troops were injured or killed.

The battle lasted for more than four months before the British called it off. The British lost 420,000 troops, the French lost nearly 200,000 troops, and the Germans lost 500,000 troops.

French troops at the Battle of the Somme

Indian soldiers on horses at the Battle of the Somme

Sympathy for the Enemy

Sometimes the soldiers felt sympathy for the other side. They were all experiencing the same cruel conditions. Small ceasefires had happened along the trenches during the war.

A German soldier approaches British lines with a Christmas tree, 1914

The ceasefires were usually used to bury the dead and fix damaged trenches.

During Christmas in 1914, there were some special ceasefires. There are many individual stories about this Christmas. Some Germans and Allies sang Christmas carols. Others exchanged gifts like tobacco and cake. Some even played soccer.

But after high-level officials found out, these ceasefires were banned from happening ever again.

14

The War in Poems and Books

About 17 million people were killed in WWI. There were approximately 20 million injured. When men joined the army at the start of the war, many thought it would be a great adventure. Most of them had no idea they would spend their time in the trenches, cold and wet and without hope.

A nurse writing a letter for a wounded soldier

Some famous poems and books were written about the war. Some soldiers kept diaries. The famous English poet and soldier Wilfred Owen wrote moving poems about it. The German soldier Erich Maria Remarque wrote a book called *All Quiet on the Western Front*. They are all worth reading.

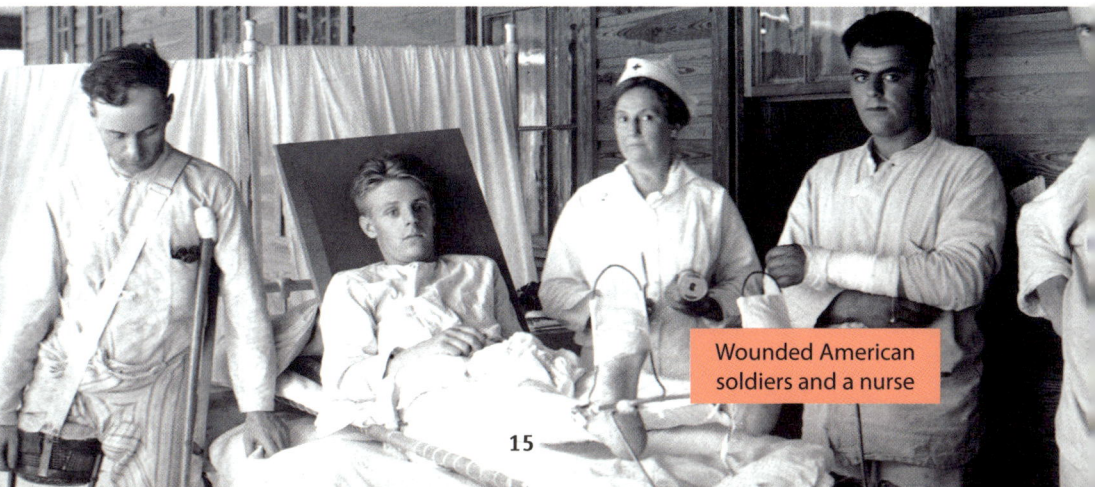

Wounded American soldiers and a nurse

The End of the War

Because the war was so brutal, it became very unpopular. There were many large anti-war demonstrations. Many people criticized their governments. Europe was in crisis.

Saint Quentin, France, in 1918, after 4 years of war

In 1917, many French soldiers refused to fight. They didn't want any more dangerous attacks against the Germans. That same year, the Russian Revolution overthrew the king in Russia. This ended Russia's participation in the war. Then in 1918, German sailors refused to fight, too. This sparked a revolution that removed the German king as well.

People all across Europe argued against the war, especially in Britain, Hungary, and Italy.

A meeting in a Russian factory during the revolution

Riots in Berlin after the war, 1919

WWI was the first to see a heavy use of planes.

Women making guns in an American factory

After five years of war, a treaty was signed in France between the Allied forces and Germany. WWI was finally over.

After WWI, war was no longer seen as something exciting and romantic. The battles in the trenches had a lot to do with that. Technology also became more important than the number of soldiers fighting a war. Many of the technologies invented in WWI became even more important in later wars. Tanks and planes became the kings of the battlefield.

During the 1920s, the countries of Europe worked to rebuild all that WWI had destroyed. But time was short. Another world war was just two decades away.

Crowds at the signing of the Treaty of Versailles, 1919

17

Comprehension Questions

1. What did many people think at the beginning of the war?
   (a) It would last for many years.
   (b) It would be over quickly.
   (c) It would be good for their economy.
   (d) They didn't know it was happening.

2. Why did the armies build trenches?
   (a) To store food
   (b) To make a place to sleep
   (c) To protect the soldiers
   (d) To collect water

3. The two sides in WWI were…
   (a) the English and the Germans.
   (b) the Allies and the Japanese.
   (c) the Allies and the Germans.
   (d) the Allies and the Central Powers.

4. How many miles of trenches were built in WWI?
   (a) Over one million
   (b) About 25,000
   (c) Around one hundred
   (d) Less than ten

5. No man's land was an area…
   (a) where no one was allowed to visit.
   (b) only for women.
   (c) between enemy trenches.
   (d) where no one could survive.

6. What was a problem soldiers in the trenches faced?
   (a) Rats
   (b) Trench foot
   (c) Depression
   (d) All of the above

7. A light-shell rocket would…
   (a) destroy a tank.
   (b) light up the sky at night.
   (c) travel far because it was not heavy.
   (d) be used during the day.

8. Which was NOT important for fighting during WWI?
   (a) The gas bomb
   (b) The tank
   (c) The machine gun
   (d) The horse

9. Who wrote *All Quiet on the Western Front*?
   (a) A French poet
   (b) A German soldier
   (c) A Russian king
   (d) An American sailor

10. After WWI, wars…
    (a) used more technology.
    (b) were romanticized.
    (c) always used trench warfare.
    (d) All of the above

Glossary

- **announcement** an official public statement about something

- **approximately** close to a specific number or time, but not exactly that number or time

- **artillery** large guns that are used to shoot over a great distance

- **ban** to make something illegal or not allowed

- **barbed wire** strong wire with short, sharp points on it

- **brutal** being extremely cruel or very violent

- **ceasefire** an agreement to stop fighting a war for a period of time

- **colony** a region or country that is being controlled by a more powerful country

- **crisis** a time that is very dangerous or difficult

- **enthusiasm** a feeling of interest and excitement about something

- **grenade** a small bomb thrown by hand or shot from a gun

- **interrogation** the act of questioning someone, often with force

- **mobile** able to move or be moved easily

- **spark** to cause something to start

- **sympathy** the feeling of understanding and caring about someone's problems

World History Timeline

This chart shows a rough overview of world history.
Some of the dates have been simplified.

World History Timeline

2900 BC	2800 BC	2700 BC	2600 BC	2500 BC

Narmer, Egyptian King
(c. 3000 BC)

Pyramids of Giza
(built c. 2550-2490 BC)

Cuneiform (c. 3000 BC-100 AD)

Old Egyptian Kingdom (c. 2686 BC)

2900 BC	2800 BC	2700 BC	2600 BC	2500 BC

← 5000 BC   Mesopotamia (Sumerians)

← 3100 BC   Early Dynastic Period of Egypt   Old Egyptian Kingdom

← 3650 BC   Minoan Civilization (Crete)

Early Bronze Age

2900 BC	2800 BC	2700 BC	2600 BC	2500 BC

2400 BC	2300 BC	2200 BC	2100 BC	2000 BC

Sahure, Egyptian King
(c. 2487-2475 BC)

Indus Valley
Civilization

Sargon the Great,
Akkadian King
(c. 2340-2284 BC)

Gudea of Lagash
(c. 2144-2124 BC)

Ur III Dynasty (c. 2112-2004 BC)

2400 BC	2300 BC	2200 BC	2100 BC	2000 BC

Xia Dynasty

Gutian Dynasty

Elam (Iran)

Akkadian Empire

Ur III Dynasty

Assyria (Early Period)

Middle Egyptian Kingdom

Minoan Civilization (Crete)

1st Intermediate
Period

Indus Valley Civilization (India)

2400 BC	2300 BC	2200 BC	2100 BC	2000 BC

World History Timeline

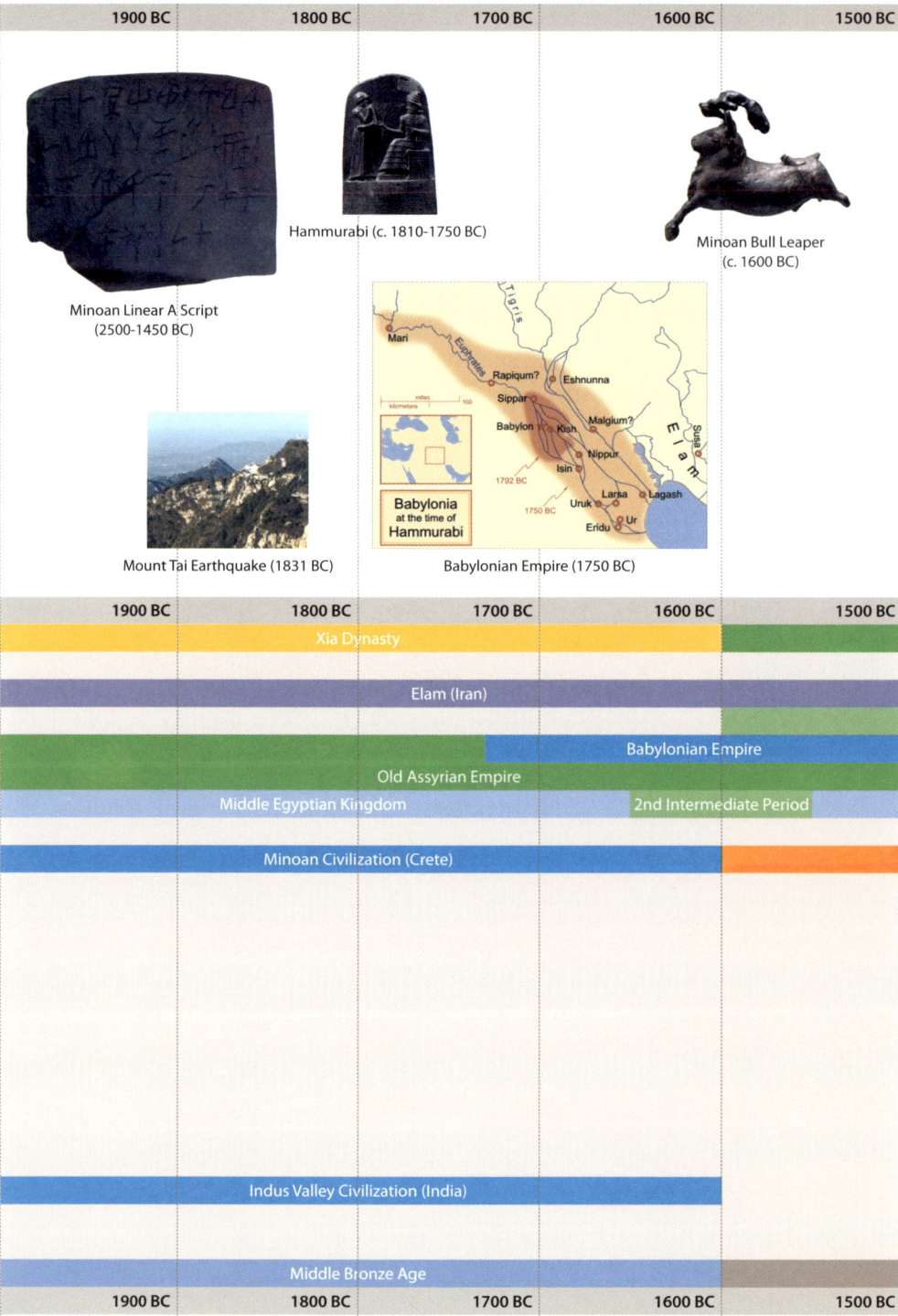

| 1900 BC | 1800 BC | 1700 BC | 1600 BC | 1500 BC |

Hammurabi (c. 1810-1750 BC)

Minoan Bull Leaper
(c. 1600 BC)

Minoan Linear A Script
(2500-1450 BC)

Mount Tai Earthquake (1831 BC)

Babylonian Empire (1750 BC)

| 1900 BC | 1800 BC | 1700 BC | 1600 BC | 1500 BC |

Xia Dynasty

Elam (Iran)

Babylonian Empire

Old Assyrian Empire

Middle Egyptian Kingdom | 2nd Intermediate Period

Minoan Civilization (Crete)

Indus Valley Civilization (India)

Middle Bronze Age

| 1900 BC | 1800 BC | 1700 BC | 1600 BC | 1500 BC |

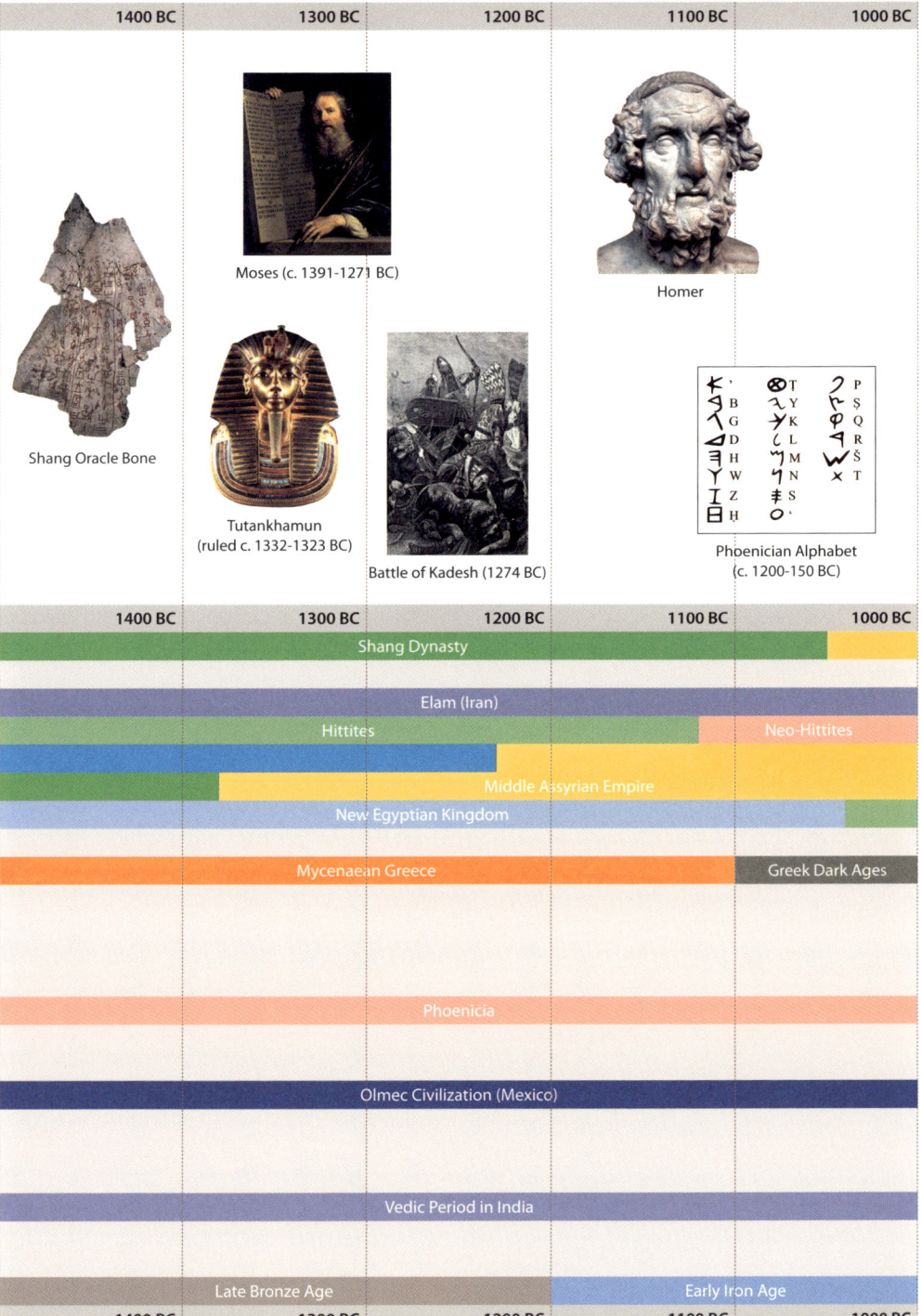

| 1400 BC | 1300 BC | 1200 BC | 1100 BC | 1000 BC |

Moses (c. 1391-1271 BC)

Homer

Shang Oracle Bone

Tutankhamun
(ruled c. 1332-1323 BC)

Battle of Kadesh (1274 BC)

Phoenician Alphabet
(c. 1200-150 BC)

| 1400 BC | 1300 BC | 1200 BC | 1100 BC | 1000 BC |

Shang Dynasty

Elam (Iran)

Hittites

Neo-Hittites

Middle Assyrian Empire

New Egyptian Kingdom

Mycenaean Greece

Greek Dark Ages

Phoenicia

Olmec Civilization (Mexico)

Vedic Period in India

Late Bronze Age

Early Iron Age

| 1400 BC | 1300 BC | 1200 BC | 1100 BC | 1000 BC |

World History Timeline

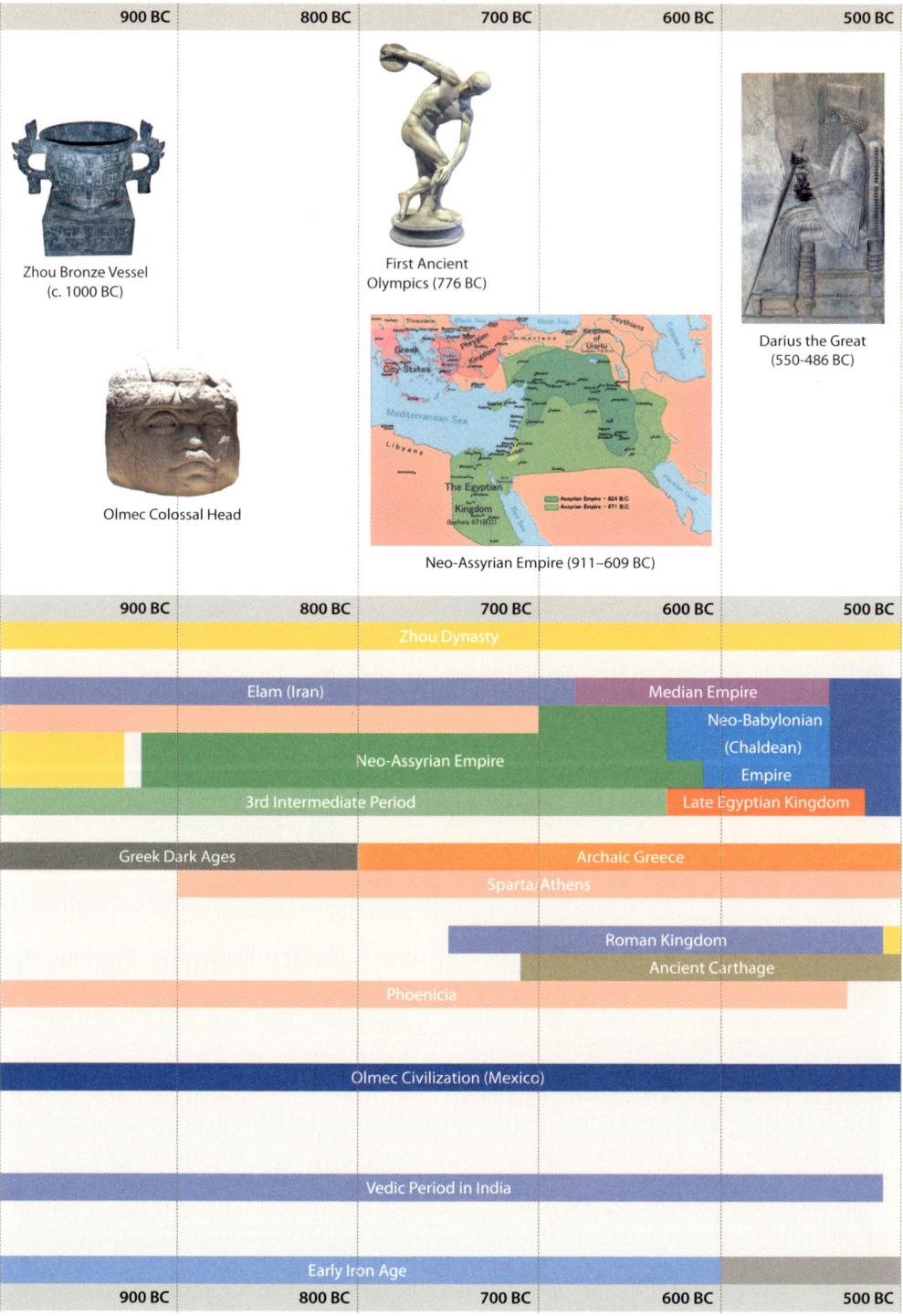

900 BC	800 BC	700 BC	600 BC	500 BC

Zhou Bronze Vessel
(c. 1000 BC)

First Ancient
Olympics (776 BC)

Darius the Great
(550-486 BC)

Olmec Colossal Head

Neo-Assyrian Empire (911–609 BC)

900 BC	800 BC	700 BC	600 BC	500 BC

Zhou Dynasty

Elam (Iran)

Median Empire

Neo-Babylonian (Chaldean) Empire

Neo-Assyrian Empire

3rd Intermediate Period

Late Egyptian Kingdom

Greek Dark Ages

Archaic Greece

Sparta/Athens

Roman Kingdom

Ancient Carthage

Phoenicia

Olmec Civilization (Mexico)

Vedic Period in India

Early Iron Age

900 BC	800 BC	700 BC	600 BC	500 BC

World History Timeline

| 400 BC | 300 BC | 200 BC | 100 BC | 0 |

Alexander the Great
(356-323 BC)

Julius Caesar
(100-44 BC)

Hannibal
(247-183 BC)

Cleopatra
(69-30 BC)

Battle of Salamis
(480 BC)

Seleucid Empire (312-63 BC)

Rossetta Stone
(created 196 BC)

| 400 BC | 300 BC | 200 BC | 100 BC | 0 |

Zhou Dynasty — Qin — Han Dynasty

Achaemenid (Persian) Empire

Alexander the Great

Parthian Empire

Seleucid Empire
Ptolemaic Kingdom
(Hellenistic Greece)

Classical Greece

Sparta/Athens

Roman Empire

Roman Republic

Roman Empire

Maurya Empire

Middle Iron Age

| 400 BC | 300 BC | 200 BC | 100 BC | 0 |

World History Timeline

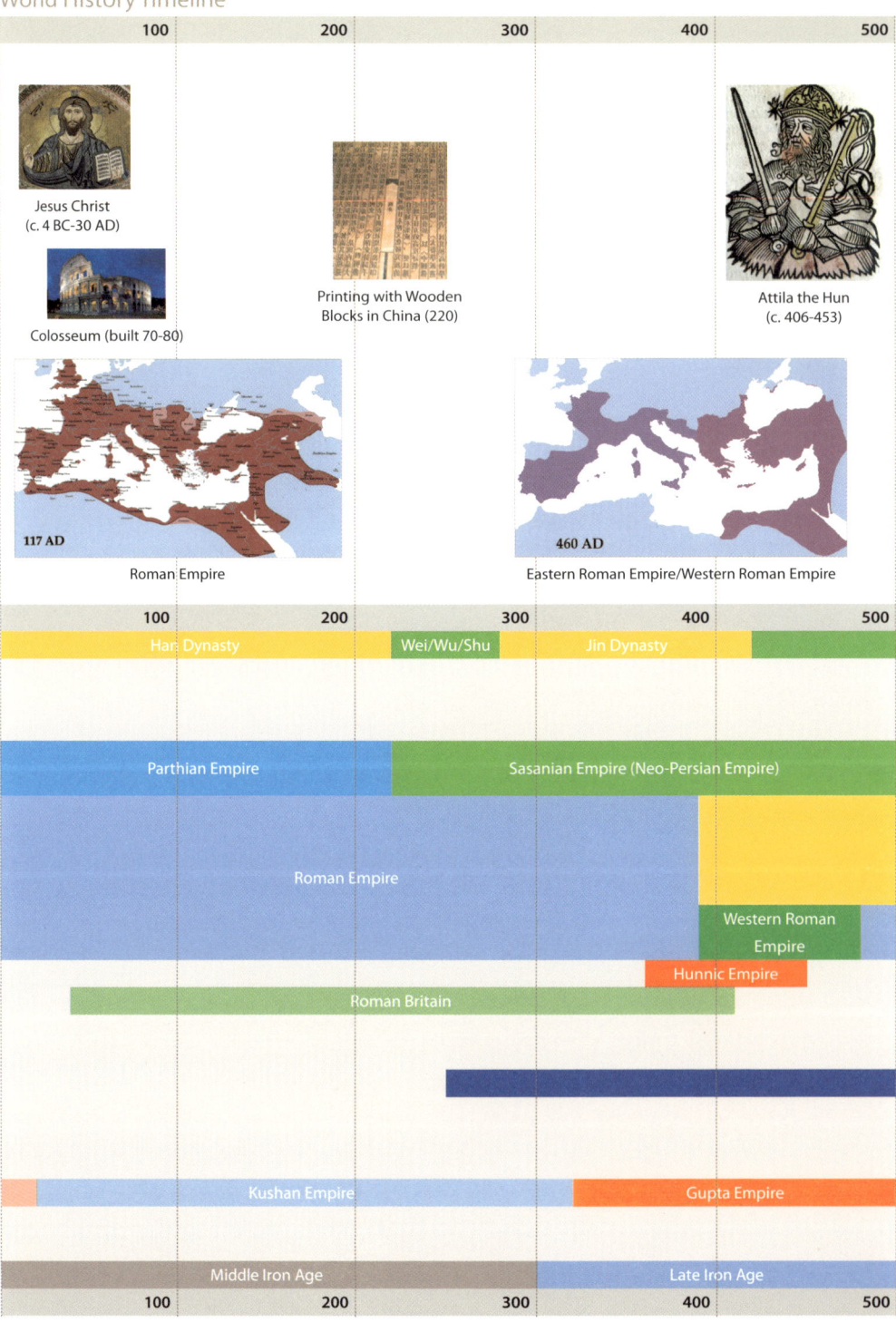

Jesus Christ
(c. 4 BC-30 AD)

Colosseum (built 70-80)

Printing with Wooden
Blocks in China (220)

Attila the Hun
(c. 406-453)

117 AD
Roman Empire

460 AD
Eastern Roman Empire/Western Roman Empire

100	200	300	400	500

Han Dynasty

Wei/Wu/Shu

Jin Dynasty

Parthian Empire

Sasanian Empire (Neo-Persian Empire)

Roman Empire

Western Roman Empire

Hunnic Empire

Roman Britain

Kushan Empire

Gupta Empire

Middle Iron Age

Late Iron Age

100	200	300	400	500

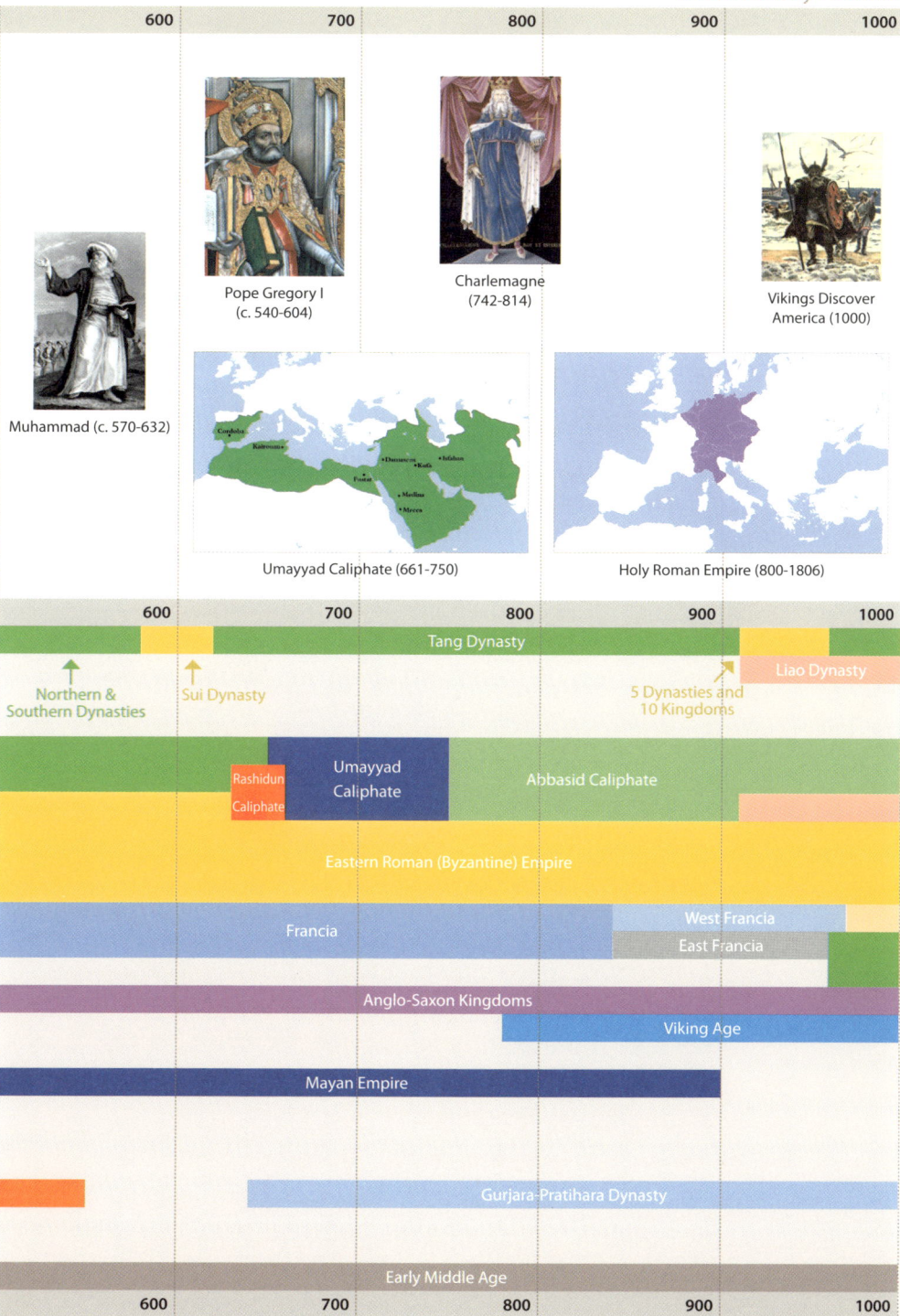

| 600 | 700 | 800 | 900 | 1000 |

Muhammad (c. 570-632)

Pope Gregory I
(c. 540-604)

Charlemagne
(742-814)

Vikings Discover
America (1000)

Umayyad Caliphate (661-750)

Holy Roman Empire (800-1806)

| 600 | 700 | 800 | 900 | 1000 |

Tang Dynasty

Liao Dynasty

Northern &
Southern Dynasties

Sui Dynasty

5 Dynasties and
10 Kingdoms

Rashidun
Caliphate

Umayyad
Caliphate

Abbasid Caliphate

Eastern Roman (Byzantine) Empire

Francia

West Francia

East Francia

Anglo-Saxon Kingdoms

Viking Age

Mayan Empire

Gurjara-Pratihara Dynasty

Early Middle Age

| 600 | 700 | 800 | 900 | 1000 |

World History Timeline

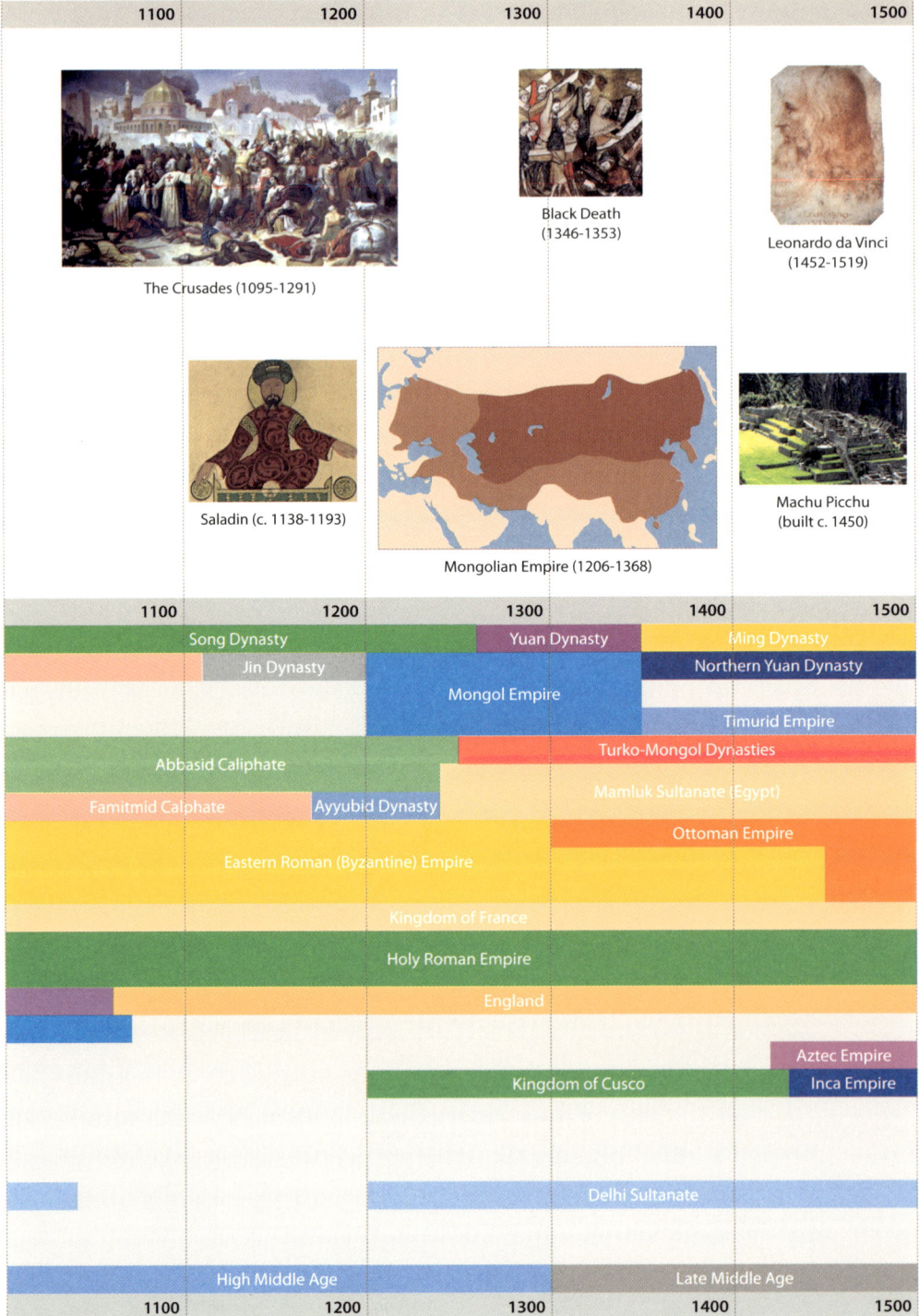

1100	1200	1300	1400	1500

The Crusades (1095-1291)

Black Death (1346-1353)

Leonardo da Vinci (1452-1519)

Saladin (c. 1138-1193)

Mongolian Empire (1206-1368)

Machu Picchu (built c. 1450)

1100	1200	1300	1400	1500

Song Dynasty

Yuan Dynasty

Ming Dynasty

Jin Dynasty

Northern Yuan Dynasty

Mongol Empire

Timurid Empire

Abbasid Caliphate

Turko-Mongol Dynasties

Famitmid Caliphate

Ayyubid Dynasty

Mamluk Sultanate (Egypt)

Eastern Roman (Byzantine) Empire

Ottoman Empire

Kingdom of France

Holy Roman Empire

England

Aztec Empire

Kingdom of Cusco

Inca Empire

Delhi Sultanate

High Middle Age

Late Middle Age

1100	1200	1300	1400	1500

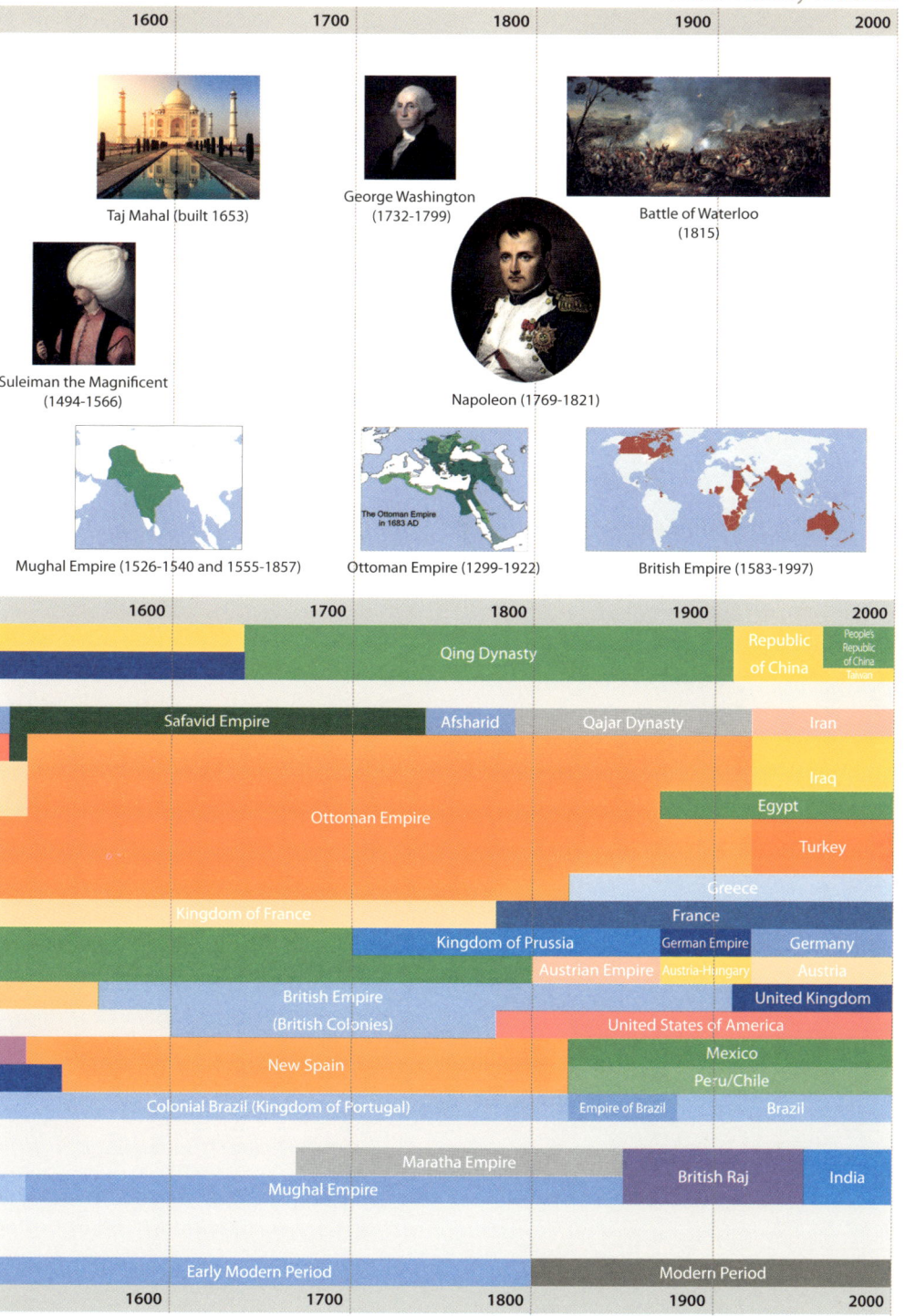

World History Timeline

| 1600 | 1700 | 1800 | 1900 | 2000 |

Taj Mahal (built 1653)

George Washington (1732-1799)

Battle of Waterloo (1815)

Suleiman the Magnificent (1494-1566)

Napoleon (1769-1821)

Mughal Empire (1526-1540 and 1555-1857)

The Ottoman Empire in 1683 AD

Ottoman Empire (1299-1922)

British Empire (1583-1997)

| 1600 | 1700 | 1800 | 1900 | 2000 |

Qing Dynasty — Republic of China — People's Republic of China / Taiwan

Safavid Empire — Afsharid — Qajar Dynasty — Iran

Iraq

Egypt

Ottoman Empire — Turkey

Greece

Kingdom of France — France

Kingdom of Prussia — German Empire — Germany

Austrian Empire — Austria-Hungary — Austria

British Empire — United Kingdom

(British Colonies) — United States of America

New Spain — Mexico

Peru/Chile

Colonial Brazil (Kingdom of Portugal) — Empire of Brazil — Brazil

Maratha Empire — British Raj — India

Mughal Empire

Early Modern Period — Modern Period

| 1600 | 1700 | 1800 | 1900 | 2000 |

List of Books